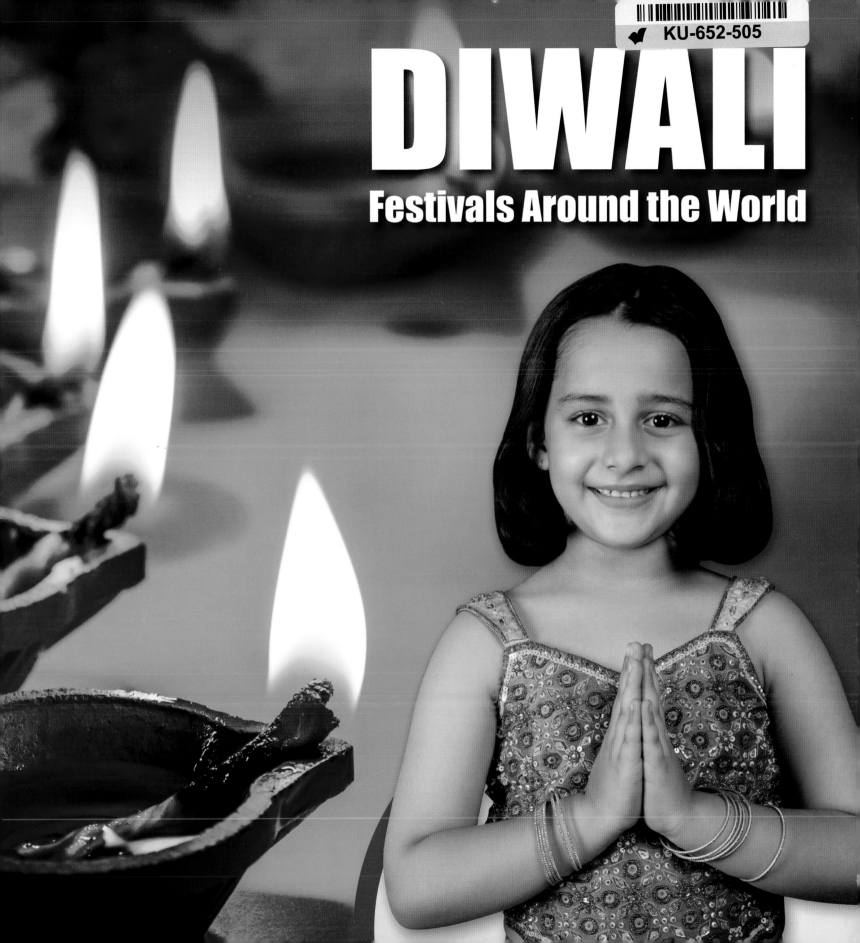

DIWALI
Festivals Around the World

Words that look like **this** can be found in the glossary on page 24.

THE SECRET BOOK COMPANY

©2019
The Secret Book
Company
King's Lynn
Norfolk PE30 4LS

ISBN: 978-1-78998-042-4

Written by:
Grace Jones
Edited by:
Charlie Ogden
Designed by:
Matt Rumbelow

A catalogue record for this book
is available from the British Library.

Diwali

Festivals Around the World

Hello, my name is Prita.

When you see Prita, she will tell you how to say a word.

What Is a Festival?

A festival takes place when people come together to celebrate a special event or time of the year. Some festivals last for only one day and others can go on for many months.

Some people celebrate festivals by having a party with their family and friends. Others celebrate by holding special events, performing dances or playing music.

What Is Hinduism?

Hinduism is a **religion** that began in India over 4,000 years ago. Hindus believe in one **supreme** god called Brahman. They pray to many different gods and goddesses who they believe are forms of Brahman.

Prita says:
BRA-MUN (Brahman)

This is Ganesh, one of the Hindu gods

Hindus can pray to their different gods and goddesses in a temple, which can also be called a mandir. Before they enter a mandir, each person must wash so they are clean and remove their shoes. This shows **respect.**

What Is Diwali?

Diwali is a festival that is celebrated by Hindus in October or November every year.

A Hindu temple in Madurai, India

Diwali celebrations usually last for five days.

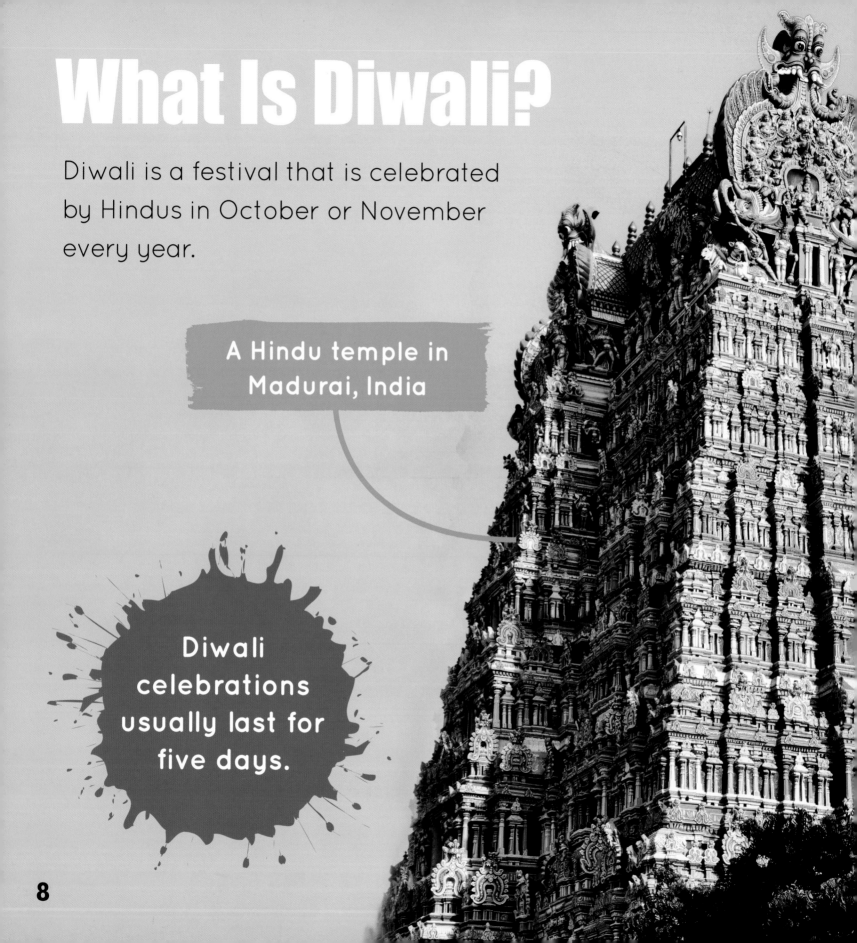

Diwali is also known as the festival of lights.

Hindus come together to celebrate good over bad. They celebrate by decorating their homes with many lights, exchanging gifts and setting off fireworks.

The Story of Diwali

A long, long time ago in India, there once was a prince called Rama who was married to a beautiful princess, Sita. Rama had an evil stepmother who wanted her son to become king instead of Rama. She sent Rama and Sita away to live in the forest.

Ravana was a demon king that had 10 heads. He had heard of Sita's beauty and wanted to make her his wife. One day, he came to the forest and took her far away to his island. Rama was sad and did not know what to do. He met Hanuman, the monkey god, in the forest and asked him for help.

Rama and Hanuman went to Ravana's island to find Sita. When they found Ravana, they had a very long and very hard battle with him. Finally, Rama shot a golden arrow that hit and killed Ravana. Rama and Sita were together once more.

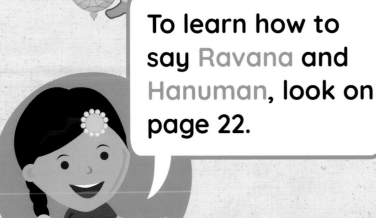

To learn how to say Ravana and Hanuman, look on page 22.

Rama and Sita tried to find their way home, but it was too dark. To help them, the people of the kingdom lit oil lamps so they could see. Rama and Sita finally came home and took their rightful place as king and queen.

Festival of Lights

During Diwali, Hindus light small oil lamps to remember the story of Rama's **faith** and good winning over evil.

The small candles lit at Diwali are called diyas.

Diya

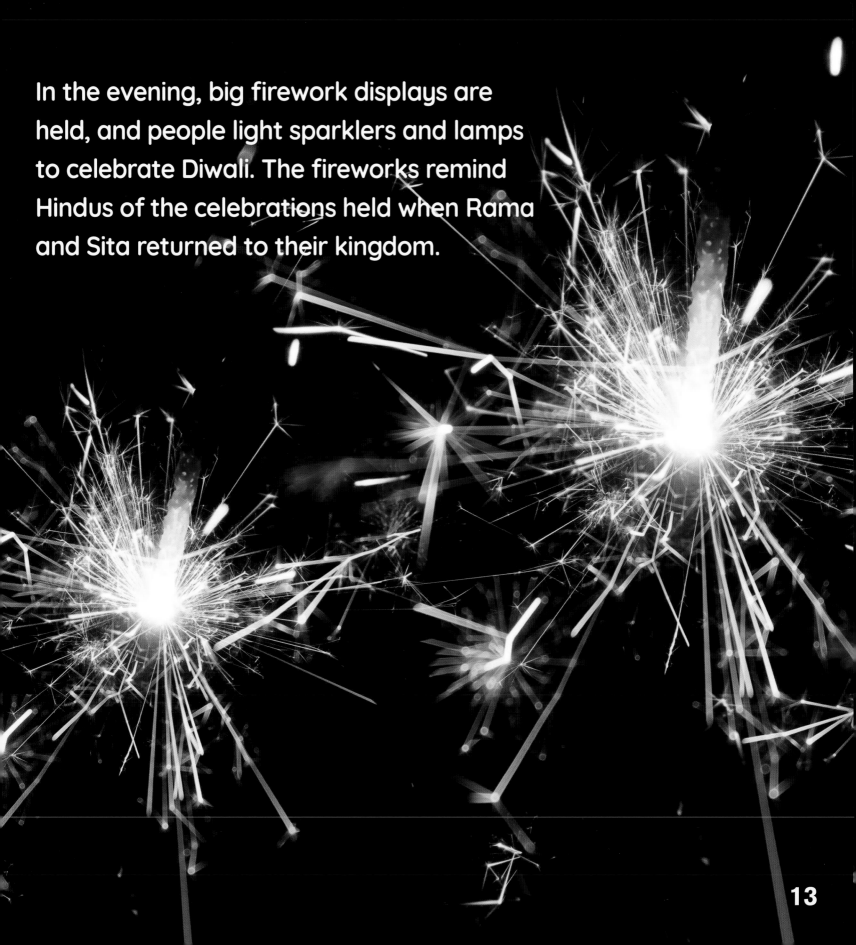

In the evening, big firework displays are held, and people light sparklers and lamps to celebrate Diwali. The fireworks remind Hindus of the celebrations held when Rama and Sita returned to their kingdom.

Prayer

Throughout the year, Hindus can hold small prayer meetings called puja. During Diwali, Hindus might pray to the god Ganesh and the goddess Lakshmi. Ganesh is the god of wisdom and good luck, and Lakshmi is the goddess of wealth and good fortune.

Lakshmi

Ganesh

Prita says:
LUK-SHMEE (Lakshmi)
GUH-NESH (Ganesh)

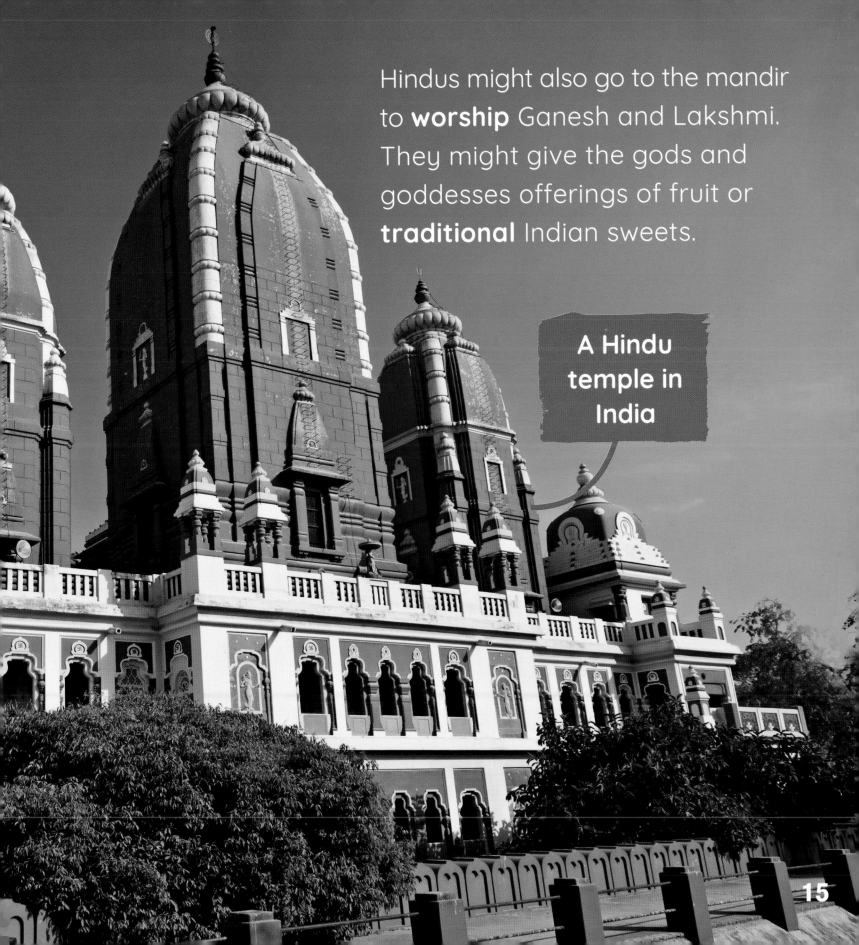

Hindus might also go to the mandir to **worship** Ganesh and Lakshmi. They might give the gods and goddesses offerings of fruit or **traditional** Indian sweets.

A Hindu temple in India

Rangoli Decorations

People decorate the doorsteps of their houses and the ground outside the temples with brightly coloured patterns. These are called rangoli patterns. The patterns can be made using a mixture of rice flour, water and coloured powder.

A rangoli pattern

Hindus hope the goddess Lakshmi will visit their houses during Diwali. Many rangoli patterns show a lotus flower. Lakshmi is often shown holding or sitting in a lotus flower.

The Hindu goddess, Lakshmi

Lotus flower

Prita says:
RAN-GO-LEE (rangoli)

Festive Food

During Diwali, brothers might visit their sisters to give them gifts such as sweets. Traditional festival foods, especially sweets, are eaten at this time of year.

Mithai

Indian sweets, called mithai, are eaten during Diwali.

Coconut barfi are also popular during Diwali. They are small sweets made from ingredients such as coconut, milk and sugar.

Prita says:
CO-CO-NUT BUR-FEE (Coconut barfi)

Music and Dancing

Hindus often come together to play music and dance during Diwali. A traditional stick dance, called the Dandiya Raas, might be performed at Diwali and other Hindu festivals.

Traditional instruments, such as the **dholak**, might be played when performers are dancing. A dholak is a traditional hand drum. People can also blow whistles and sing during the festival.

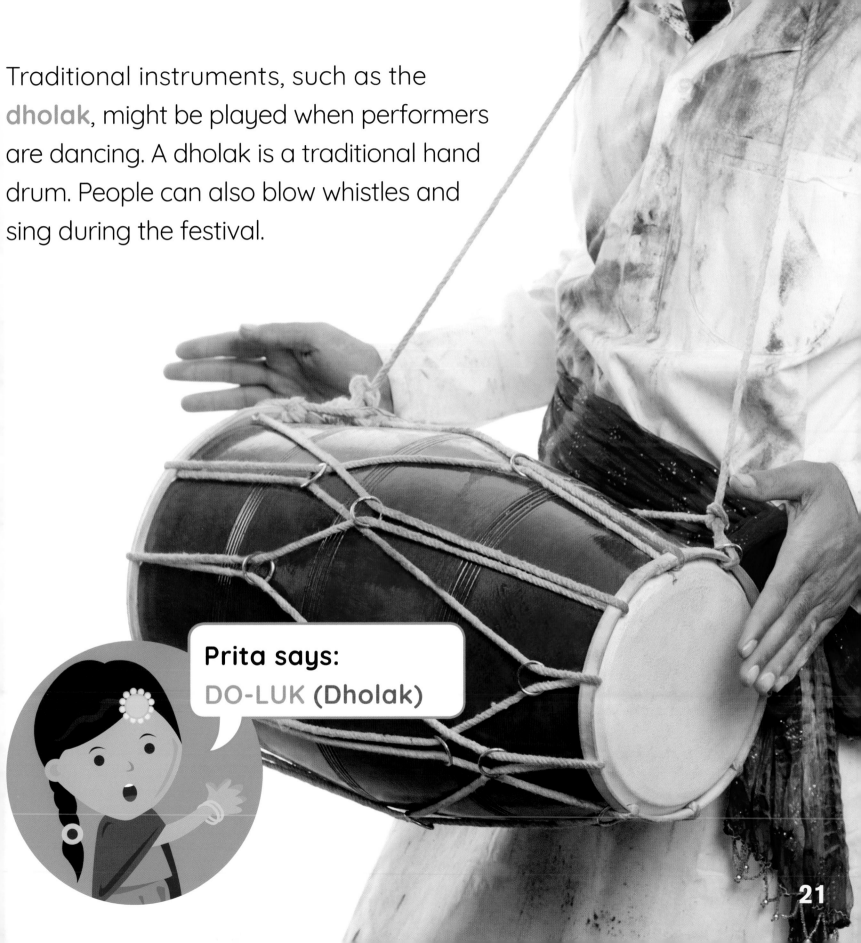

Prita says:
DO-LUK (Dholak)

Prita Says...

Brahman
BRA-MUN
The supreme Hindu god

Coconut Barfi
CO-CO-NUT BUR-FEE
Small sweets made from ingredients such as coconut, milk and sugar

Dholak
DOH-LUK
A traditional hand drum

Ganesh
GUH-NESH
The god of wisdom and good luck

Hanuman

HA-NOO-MUN

The monkey god of strength and destroyer of evil

Lakshmi

LUK-SHMEE

The goddess of wealth and good fortune

Rangoli

RAN-GO-LEE

A colourful pattern drawn during Diwali

Ravana

RA-VARN-AH

The demon king

Glossary

faith great trust in someone or something

religion a belief in a god or gods

respect feeling that something or someone is important

supreme the greatest

traditional something that is passed from person to person over a long time

worship a religious act, such as praying

Index

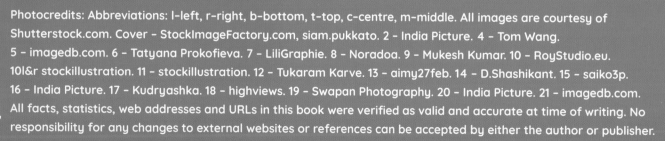

Credits

Photocredits: Abbreviations: l-left, r-right, b-bottom, t-top, c-centre, m-middle. All images are courtesy of Shutterstock.com. Cover - StockImageFactory.com, siam.pukkato. 2 - India Picture. 4 - Tom Wang. 5 - imagedb.com. 6 - Tatyana Prokofieva. 7 - LiliGraphie. 8 - Noradoa. 9 - Mukesh Kumar. 10 - RoyStudio.eu. 10l&r stockillustration. 11 - stockillustration. 12 - Tukaram Karve. 13 - aimy27feb. 14 - D.Shashikant. 15 - saiko3p. 16 - India Picture. 17 - Kudryashka. 18 - highviews. 19 - Swapan Photography. 20 - India Picture. 21 - imagedb.com. All facts, statistics, web addresses and URLs in this book were verified as valid and accurate at time of writing. No responsibility for any changes to external websites or references can be accepted by either the author or publisher.